the story of...

ALEXANDER
THE GREAT

Author
Dr Nicholas Saunders

THE CAST

Alexander III of Macedonia (Alexander the Great) *Born in July 356 BC to King Philip II and Queen Olympias at Pella. According to legend the goddess Artemis attended his birth. Clever, tough and resourceful, Alexander built the largest empire ever seen in the ancient world. It stretched from Greece to India. He died unexpectedly in Babylon in 323 at the age of 32.*

Philip II of Macedonia *Son of King Amyntas III, who became king in 359. A skilled and energetic soldier. His army reforms and string of victories transformed Macedonia into the most powerful state in Greece. Father of Alexander III (the Great). He was assassinated at Aegae in the summer of 336.*

Olympias *Sister of King Alexander of Molossia, and a royal princess. Wife of King Philip II of Macedonia and mother of Alexander III (the Great). Energetic and spiteful by nature, she was suspected of Philip's assassination. She was murdered during the chaotic wars of succession that followed Alexander's death.*

Hephaestion *Boyhood friend of Alexander who became his most intimate and life-long companion. Alexander appointed him Grand Vizier of the empire. He died unexpectedly at Ecbatana in October 324. A huge and expensive funeral was held for him in Babylon in 323, just weeks before Alexander's own death.*

Roxanne *Bactrian princess and daughter of the Sogdian ruler Oxyartes. Alexander married her in 327. She gave Alexander his only legitimate heir, Alexander IV, but both were murdered in Macedonia during the wars of succession that followed Alexander's death.*

Darius III *King of the Persian empire. He ruled from 336 until defeated (for a second time) by Alexander at the Battle of Gaugamela in 331. He fled the battlefield but was murdered by the pretender king Bessus in 330.*

Copyright © ticktock Entertainment Ltd. 2006
First published in Great Britain in 2006 by ticktock Media Ltd.,
Unit 2, Orchard Business Centre, North Farm Road, Tunbridge Wells, Kent, TN2 3XF
We would like to thank: Starry Dog Books Limited for their help with this book.
ISBN 1 84696 000 2
Printed in China
A CIP catalogue record for this book is available from the British Library.

CONTENTS

SETTING THE SCENE

Alexander the Great (Alexander III) became king of Macedonia following the violent death of his father, King Philip II, in 336 BC. He inherited a vast empire that encompassed all of Greece, controlled from Pella. Despite his tender age (Alexander was just 20 when he came to power), the new king proved himself to be a skilled leader. In just 11 years he and his army had conquered a number of countries, building the largest empire in the ancient world.

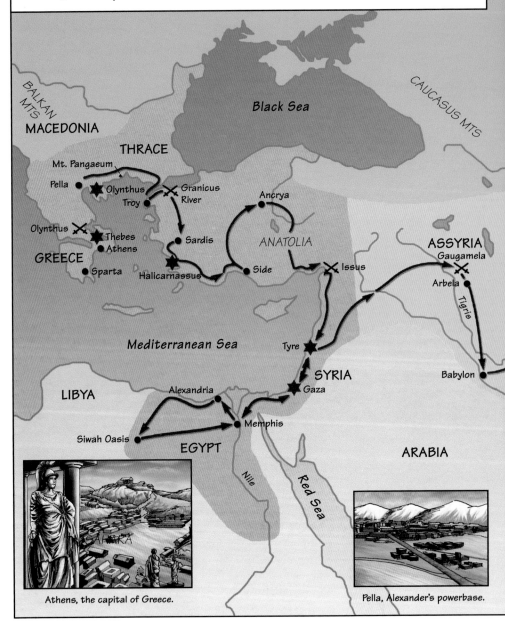

Athens, the capital of Greece.

Pella, Alexander's powerbase.

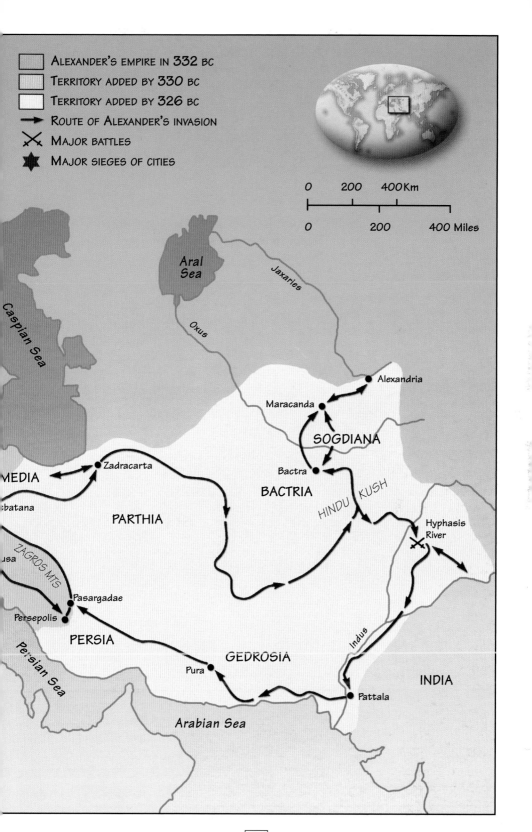

ALEXANDER'S EMPIRE IN **332** BC
TERRITORY ADDED BY **330** BC
TERRITORY ADDED BY **326** BC
ROUTE OF ALEXANDER'S INVASION
MAJOR BATTLES
MAJOR SIEGES OF CITIES

0   200   400 Km
0   200   400 Miles

Aral Sea

Jaxartes

Oxus

Caspian Sea

Alexandria

Maracanda

SOGDIANA

Bactra

MEDIA

Zadracarta

BACTRIA

HINDU KUSH

batana

PARTHIA

Hyphasis River

ZAGROS MTS

usa

Pasargadae

Persepolis

PERSIA

Indus

GEDROSIA

Pura

INDIA

Persian Sea

Pattala

Arabian Sea

A YOUNG LEADER

Alexander's early years were adventurous. The goddess Artemis was said to have overseen his birth, which was thought to be a blessing. His talent for hunting, fighting, and intelligence were quickly noticed. However, death and tragedy also played their part.

On 20th July 356 BC, Alexander was born in the royal palace at the Macedonian capital of Pella. Alexander's mother, Queen Olympias, presented the royal son to his father, King Philip.

Philip, husband, see your beautiful baby – already he has your eyes.

Alexander, my son. One day you will rule this great kingdom, and these great nobles will be at your command.

King Philip's royal nobles gathered round to see the new baby who one day would become King of Macedonia.

At the same time as Alexander was born, the Temple of Artemis in the great city of Ephesus was destroyed by a violent earthquake.

King Philip and his generals fought hard and partied hard at Pella after a military victory.

Under your leadership, we will conquer the whole of Greece and Persia!

Drink and eat my generals, for we have won another famous victory!

Oh spirit of Dionysus, protect my son Alexander, and make him Lord of Asia!

Queen Olympias was devoted to the Cult of Dionysus. She especially liked magic rituals which involved handling snakes.

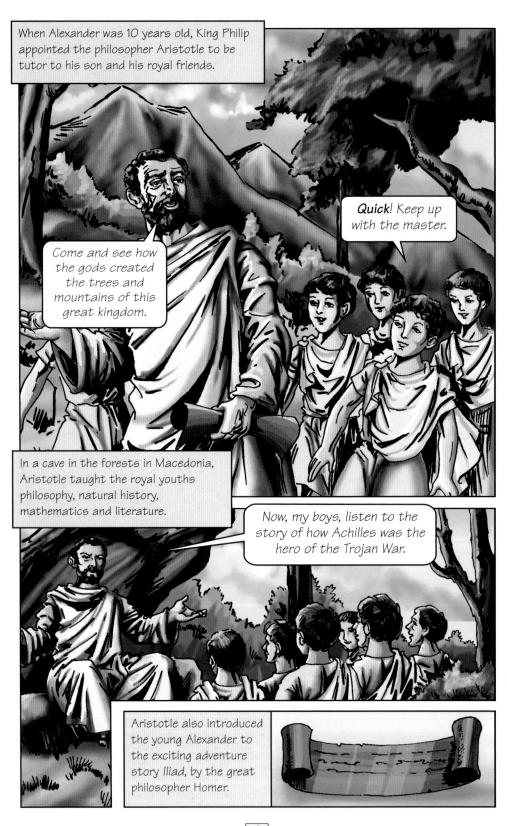

When Alexander was 10 years old, King Philip appointed the philosopher Aristotle to be tutor to his son and his royal friends.

Come and see how the gods created the trees and mountains of this great kingdom.

Quick! Keep up with the master.

In a cave in the forests in Macedonia, Aristotle taught the royal youths philosophy, natural history, mathematics and literature.

Now, my boys, listen to the story of how Achilles was the hero of the Trojan War.

Aristotle also introduced the young Alexander to the exciting adventure story Iliad, by the great philosopher Homer.

In the palace at Pella, the young Alexander met Hephaestion for the first time. The two boys quickly became inseparable friends, developing a lifelong relationship.

Greetings Hephaestion. I am Alexander, son of King Philip. Welcome to my father's royal city.

Thank you! I have heard so much about you. Perhaps we can be friends?

Alexander and Hephaestion hunted wild boar together. They learnt skills they would use later when they hunted lions in Macedonia.

Watch out Alexander! It may turn and charge your horse. Shoot it now!

Quick! Hephaestion – it's getting away. Throw your spear and I'll shoot my arrow.

FAST FACT

In Alexander's time there were no books. Scrolls of parchment or papyrus were used instead, and rolled up to keep safe.

The Macedonian cavalry was made up of noblemen who could afford to own and keep horses on their country estates. They trained constantly, and were regarded as the best cavalry in the ancient world.

When Alexander was 12 years old, he watched his father's horse trainers struggling to tame an expensive wild stallion. Despite their strength and experience, the men were unable to control the horse, called Bucephalus.

Watch father! I'll mount and tame this stallion.

Careful boy! He'll throw you right off.

Alexander noticed that Bucephalus was spooked by his own shadow. He approached with the sun behind him then jumped on the horse's back and rode it across the plain.

Despite his youth, Alexander mastered Bucephalus. King Philip was so proud that he bought the horse for his son.

You did it son! Macedonia is too small a kingdom for the likes of you. I'll buy Bucephalus whatever the cost – the horse is yours.

FAST FACT

Macedonian horses were small. They were not fitted with horseshoes, and stirrups had not yet been invented.

When Alexander was 16 years old, his father Philip named him regent. This meant that Alexander was next-in-line. Philip went away on a campaign, leaving Alexander in charge.

Despite superior numbers and familiarity with the countryside, the Maedi were out-fought and out-manoeuvered by Alexander's men.

Grrrrr!

Push them forward with your spears! They will give way!

Macedonian battle tactics and strict discipline allowed Alexander to destroy the brave but reckless and disorganized Maedi.

As a sign of things to come, Alexander celebrated his victory by founding his own town on the ruins of the old Maedi capital.

We have won a great victory Macedonians! To celebrate, I proclaim this to be my first city, Alexandropolis.

Alexandropolis in Thrace was Alexander's first self-named town. He would found or re-name dozens of others during a lifetime of conquests across Asia.

FAST FACT

Fighting the wild tribes of the Maedi and Illyrians on Macedonia's northern borders sharpened the military skills that Alexander would use in winning an empire.

Next, Alexander faced brave Theban warriors known as the Sacred Band, who vowed to fight to the death.

Stand firm Thebans. We shall defeat the Macedonians.

Macedonians look! We shall fight the Thebans. The bravest of warriors!

In 338 BC, the 18-year old Alexander was given command of the elite Companion Cavalry. He led the troups to fight against Athens and her Theban allies at the Battle of Chaeronea in central Greece.

Flee brothers. Alexander is upon us!

Charge! For Philip and Macedonia.

Kill!

Alexander's brilliant cavalry charge broke the Greek line and threw the Greeks into confusion. Many died as they ran from the battlefield.

The battle was hard. Alexander jumped off his horse and fought a bitter hand-to-hand struggle with the Thebans. At last, the Macedonians gained the edge.

Surrender Theban! All is lost. The gods are against you! I will win this battle. Surrender now!

Arrgggh!

Athens and her allies suffered a terrible defeat. Philip congratulated his son and gave him the honour of returning the Athenian dead to Athens for burial.

King Philip, we the Greeks surrender to you and your mighty son.

Alexander my son. **Your** charge won the battle.

To honour the dead warriors, a giant funerary monument was erected. It was a great lion, made from white marble, that stood guard over the graves.

A NEW KING

Alexander's reputation was made in the years 336-331 BC. He defeated Persian forces at the Battle of the Granicus river, besieged the great city of Halicarnassus, crushed Darius at Issus and the captured the island city of Tyre. He captured Egypt where he was proclaimed pharaoh, and built the city of Alexandria.

Stay here Alexander. As father of the bride, I must enter the arena alone to be welcomed by the audience.

In the summer of 336 BC, Philip entered the theatre at Aegae with Alexander. His daughter Cleopatra was celebrating her marriage to the king of neighbouring Epirus.

Entering the arena alone, Philip was killed by his bodyguard Pausanias.

Die Philip! This is for the insults I have suffered and you have ignored.

Aaagh! Traitor! Traitor!

Quick, quick – don't let the assassin escape. He has killed the king!

Die traitor!

Aaagh!

Pausanias galloped away on a horse which had been left nearby. He was quickly chased by the other bodyguards.

Before Pausanias could speak, the other bodyguards stabbed him to death.

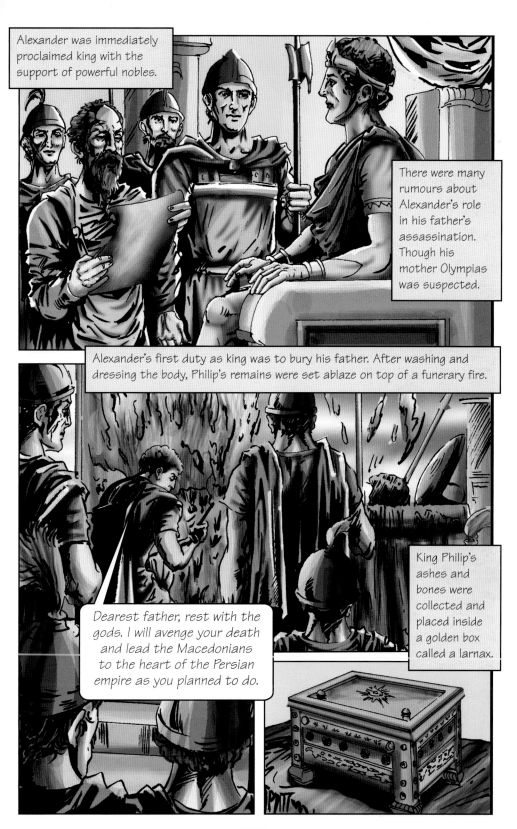

Alexander was immediately proclaimed king with the support of powerful nobles.

There were many rumours about Alexander's role in his father's assassination. Though his mother Olympias was suspected.

Alexander's first duty as king was to bury his father. After washing and dressing the body, Philip's remains were set ablaze on top of a funerary fire.

King Philip's ashes and bones were collected and placed inside a golden box called a larnax.

Dearest father, rest with the gods. I will avenge your death and lead the Macedonians to the heart of the Persian empire as you planned to do.

In the spring of 334 BC, the Macedonians invaded the Persian empire. Alexander was the first to jump ashore.

Hurrah! Alexander will conquer Persia!

I claim this land in the name of the gods.

Athena, goddess of war. I dedicate my armour to you.

Quick, Macedonians. Across the river and charge the enemy.

Stand fast! The river will protect us.

Alexander dedicated his armour to Athena at her shrine near Troy. He took the armour of the hero Achilles in exchange.

In May, Alexander was victorious in his first battle against the Persians and their Greek allies, who were hired to fight with them. At the battle of the River Granicus Alexander's life was saved by the Macedonian noble Cleitus the Black.

Alexander laid siege to the city of Halicarnassus between August and September 334 BC. He lost many men, but finally stormed through the city's great walls.

Attack the gate, it is giving way. We will rush them there.

In 333 BC, in Phrygia, Alexander was challenged to undo the tangled Gordion Knot by the prediction that whoever did so would conquer Asia. Alexander slashed the knot in half.

Alexander and his general Ptolemy stood in amazement before the huge burial Mausoleum to King Mausolus.

Sir, Mausolus was a nobody. Your tomb will be even greater!

FAST FACT The Mausoleum at Halicarnassus stood 60 metres tall, and was built of limestone. At its summit was a statue of Mausolus driving a chariot. It was one of the Seven Wonders of the World.

THE BATTLE OF ISSUS

In November of 333 BC, Alexander fought the Persian King Darius III on the coastal plains of Issus in Cilicia (southern Turkey). Despite being outnumbered, the Macedonians beat the Persians.

Alexander besieged the island fortress city of Tyre between January and August 332 BC. The Tyrians believed themselves safe behind their massive sheer walls, and inflicted many casualties on the Macedonians.

Alexander won the day when he charged furiously at Darius's chariot. The Persian king fled in panic, and the Macedonians captured his headquarters, golden treasures, and even Darius's mother Queen Sisygambis.

Majesty, we are cut off! We must retreat. You must escape to fight again!

Alexander. You shall pay for invading my empire!

Alexander built a great road from the shore to the island and stormed the city. His men slaughtered many soldiers, crucified prisoners, and enslaved the survivors.

By Herakles! We will take Tyre and burn it to the ground!

FAST FACT

Alexander's determination to conquer Tyre, and his inventive genius at building the causeway added awe and respect to his reputation as a brilliant general. It spread fear across Asia.

21

In November 332 BC, Alexander and his army entered Egypt, defeating the small Persian garrison there. They were amazed by the huge pyramids at Giza, and gazed in wonder at the mysterious stone face of the Sphinx.

Sir, this sphinx I am told was made for a pharaoh.

What gods are these Hephaestion? Surely no man could build such gigantic monuments!

Hail Alexander! We welcome you as our country's saviour from the Persians. You are truly the new pharoah.

Alexander journeyed to the Egyptian capital at Memphis. Here he was welcomed by the powerful Egyptian priesthood and made a new pharaoh.

Early in 331 BC, Alexander's men rode across the Egyptian desert to reach the Oracle Temple of the god Ammon at Siwa. They were guided there by a flock of birds.

Quickly! Follow the birds. They are a sign from the gods and will guide us to Siwa.

Alexander and his men arrived safely at the Siwa oasis. Alexander walked towards the Oracle Temple to hear what the god Ammon predicted for his future.

The chief priest welcomed Alexander as the son of Ammon. Alexander was keen to be known as a living god. It was talked about across the ancient world.

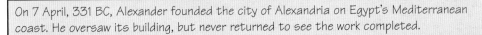

On 7 April, 331 BC, Alexander founded the city of Alexandria on Egypt's Mediterranean coast. He oversaw its building, but never returned to see the work completed.

THE BATTLE OF GAUGAMELA

In 331 BC, King Darius III and Alexander met again. Darius chose a wide, open plain near the village of Gaugamela for this battle. He led his army from Babylon, and waited for Alexander. In September of 331 BC, Alexander and 47,000 of his Macedonian troops arrived at Gaugamela.

We fight tomorrow. Do not fear that we are outnumbered – there may be more men standing on their side, but there will be more spirit fighting on ours!

The scouts say there are five of them for each one of us.

I hear that a ram has been sacrificed to the gods. The omens say we will win the battle.

I heard that the Persians have got strange monsters to help them. They've got hundreds of chariots, too.

The first fighting was between Alexander's cavalry and Darius' horsemen.

Darius used Indian elephants in the battle to scare Alexander's horses. Alexander's cavalry was smaller than the Persians, but they held off Darius's horsemen.

Fight horseman, fight! We are losing too many men.

The horses are terrified by the great beasts, sir.

The Persian army had 200 war chariots with razor-sharp blades sticking out from the axles of their wheels. The chariots charged across the plain towards the Macedonian lines.

Use your bows and spears to kill the chariot drivers.

When a Persian chariot driver was killed or injured, the Macedonian soldiers caught the horses and chariots. Trained war horses were a good battle prize!

Sir, Hephaestion has been wounded.

Alexander's closest friend Hephaestion was slashed on the arm by a spear.

Doctors waited behind the battle lines to treat the injured.

Send my own doctor, Philip of Acarnania, to help him. Let me know how he gets on.

The fighting continued for many hours. Alexander and his men fought their way closer and closer to Darius's camp.

Sir! Look! A gap has opened in the Persian lines of defence.

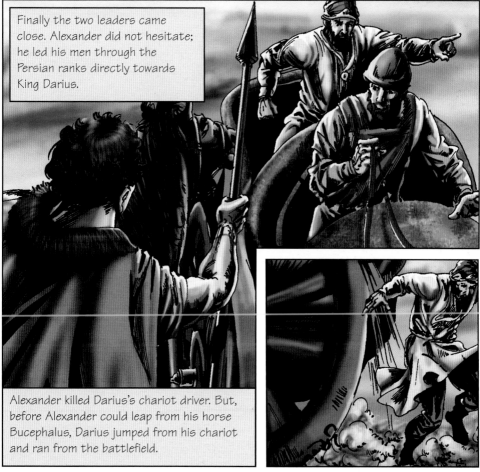

Finally the two leaders came close. Alexander did not hesitate; he led his men through the Persian ranks directly towards King Darius.

Alexander killed Darius's chariot driver. But, before Alexander could leap from his horse Bucephalus, Darius jumped from his chariot and ran from the battlefield.

In October 331 BC, Alexander's army marched south and entered the great city of Babylon through its magnificent Ishtar Gate.

We will enter Babylon through the Ishtar Gate and take control of the city.

Alexander and his men stood amazed at the great stepped temple of Babylon's god Marduk which towered above the city.

Mighty Marduk! Never before have I seen such a temple reaching to the sky!

As Babylon's new master, Alexander ordered that the city's treasury be taken.

Seize the treasury! All Persian gold belongs to me!

Alexander arrived at the sacred Persian capital of Persepolis (in central Iran) in the spring of 330 BC. He found a magnificent city containing another vast treasury of gold and silver.

Another hoard of Persian treasure that is now ours. I will use it to pay my soldiers.

In April after a great banquet, urged on by his men, Alexander set fire to the Great Palace.

May the gods be pleased! Let us sacrifice the Persian capital to the flames!

Alexander paid his respects to Cyrus the Great, the founder of the Persian empire, at his tomb at Pasargadae.

ALEXANDER IN INDIA

In the spring of 329 BC, Alexander led his army across the snowy mountains of the Hindu Kush in Afghanistan. He was heading for Bactria, chasing after the Persian pretender king Bessus. He paid off his older soldiers and sent them home.

Forward Macedonians. We must capture Bessus even if we follow him beyond the sky mountains.

Where are we heading? No man can cross these mountains!

Alexander's general Ptolemy captured Bessus who was later murdered. Alexander crossed the great river Oxus and took the chief Sogdian city of Maracanda (Samarkand). He moved north, crossed the Jaxartes river, and founded Alexandria Eschate ('the furthest').

In the spring of 327 BC, Alexander attacked the so-called indestructable fortress known as the Sogdian Rock. It belonged to the local ruler Oxyartes.

Forward Macedonians! We must take this impossible fortress!

After the capture of the Sogdian Rock, Alexander married Oxyartes's daughter, the beautiful Bactrian princess Roxanne. Although the alliance had political benefits, the marriage was said to be a loving one.

Roxanne — you shall be my queen and mother of my heir.

Sir, I will and I will love you too.

Late in 327 BC, Alexander re-crossed the Hindu Kush, and led his army through the Khyber Pass and down into lush plains below. The invasion of India had begun.

At last we leave the cold mountains and welcome the heat of India. Here there are new enemies to conquer.

In May 326 BC, Alexander finally confronted the mighty army of the Indian Rajah Porus. He organized his Companion Cavalry and his infantry to face the enemy.

Quick! We must stop Porus's advance!

The Macedonians saw for the first time the vast size of Porus's forces: 30,000 infantry, 4,000 cavalry, 1,000 war chariots and 200 war elephants.

Look Macedonians! The Indian army is like a sea of men.

Macedonians! Shields together and spears held high!

The Macedonians were astonished to see the Rajah Porus. He was a giant of a man with massive ranks of armoured war elephants.

Sir, see the enemy run. They are scared of your elephants.

We must be careful. This Alexander has a fearsome reputation.

FAST FACT Indian elephants are smaller and more easily tamed than African ones. Two men sat on each elepheant. One threw spears and fired arrows at the Macedonians while the other controlled the beast.

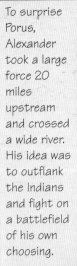

To surprise Porus, Alexander took a large force 20 miles upstream and crossed a wide river. His idea was to outflank the Indians and fight on a battlefield of his own choosing.

We must cross the river before Porus discovers our trick!

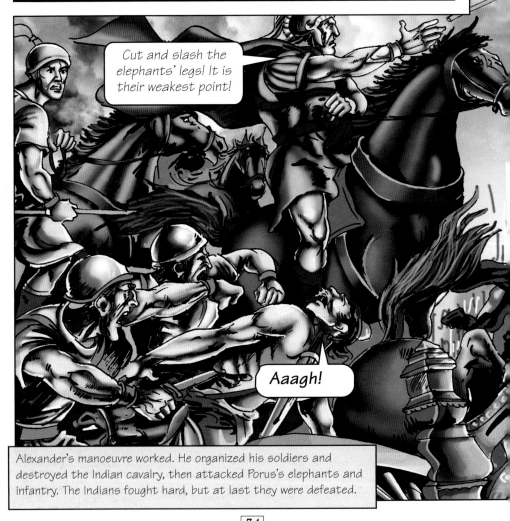

Cut and slash the elephants' legs! It is their weakest point!

Aaagh!

Alexander's manoeuvre worked. He organized his soldiers and destroyed the Indian cavalry, then attacked Porus's elephants and infantry. The Indians fought hard, but at last they were defeated.

Porus refused to surrender and fought bravely to the end. Alexander sent ambassadors to request his surrender, which he finally agreed to. Alexander made the Rajah an ally and allowed him to retain his kingdom.

I must shoot Alexander. If he is killed the Macedonians will be defeated.

Alexander's horse Bucephalus was mortally wounded during the battle. Alexander founded a city in the horse's honour, and named it Bucephala.

Bucephalus – my faithful horse since childhood. Now you will gallop on the Elysian Fields.

THE FINAL YEARS

After conquering Porus, Alexander's army mutinied when he ordered them to go further into India. Alexander nearly died from an Indian arrow shot, a disastrous desert crossing left tens of thousands dead, and the army mutinied a second time at Opis. Alexander's dearest friend, Hephaestion, died in October 324 BC. Alexander himself died just a few months later in June 323 BC.

In June 326 BC, Alexander marched the victorious army east to the Hyphasis (Beas) river. Here, the army mutinied. They had fought for 8 years with no end in sight. Alexander decided he would return to Babylon.

Many of Alexander's soldiers were over 60, and had fought with King Philip. All now wanted to enjoy their lives. They did not want to continue fighting for Alexander's personal glory.

Alexander led his army back to the Hydaspes river where his carpenters began building a fleet of ships that would transport them downriver to the Indian Ocean.

In early 325 BC, Alexander attacked a town belonging to the Malli tribe. He was trapped and near fatally wounded, but eventually recovered from his wounds.

FAST FACT Alexander's relentless advance into India was only stopped by the mutiny of his own men. Before he turned back, Alexander had 12 huge altars made – one for each of the Greek Olympian gods.

From November 326 until August 325 BC, Alexander and his fleet sailed down the Hydaspes and Indus rivers until they reached Pattala. From here, Alexander began his crossing of the Gedrosian desert, and his admiral Nearchus sailed out into the Indian ocean.

Alexander marched across the Gedrosian desert (in southern Iran) for 60 days. It was so hot that Alexander and his army had to march by night. Supplies failed to appear, and water and food ran dangerously low.

Thousands of soldiers, women, and children died of thirst and had to be left behind unburied. By the time Alexander emerged from the desert he had lost perhaps 60,000 lives of his original 85,000. It was the biggest disaster of his life.

Leave me wife, I cannot go on. Save yourself and our child.

Let the desert drink this! If my army cannot drink neither shall I.

Sir, you must drink. We only have a little water left!

Alexander shared the hardships of the desert march. He walked his horse, and refused to drink water when so many others could not.

40

In the autumn of 324 BC, Alexander marched his army into the Zagros mountains to the city of Ecbatana. Here he celebrated ten years of victories in Asia with magnificent athletic games, music, and plays for his army.

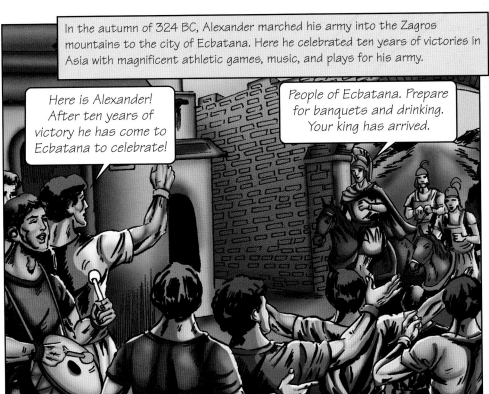

Here is Alexander! After ten years of victory he has come to Ecbatana to celebrate!

People of Ecbatana. Prepare for banquets and drinking. Your king has arrived.

In October, Hephaestion was taken ill during a banquet and died. Alexander was heartbroken.

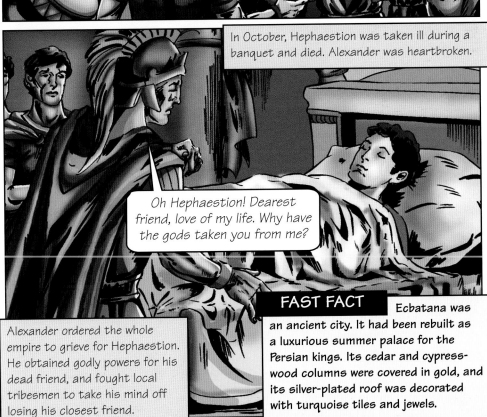

Oh Hephaestion! Dearest friend, love of my life. Why have the gods taken you from me?

Alexander ordered the whole empire to grieve for Hephaestion. He obtained godly powers for his dead friend, and fought local tribesmen to take his mind off losing his closest friend.

FAST FACT Ecbatana was an ancient city. It had been rebuilt as a luxurious summer palace for the Persian kings. Its cedar and cypress-wood columns were covered in gold, and its silver-plated roof was decorated with turquoise tiles and jewels.

Alexander returned to Babylon in early 323 BC to bury his friend and to plan for an invasion of Arabia. Banquets paid for from the riches of Asia were held almost every night.

On his deathbed, Alexander called his general and friends around him. He gave his royal signet ring to Perdiccas, the empire's Grand Vizier, but added that the empire would go to the strongest man.

Alexander is dying. He will soon be with his spiritual father, Ammon.

Lord, I am honoured. I will protect Roxanne and your son. He shall succeed you!

Perdiccas, take my royal ring. You shall prevent chaos for now. For the future I predict great funeral games.

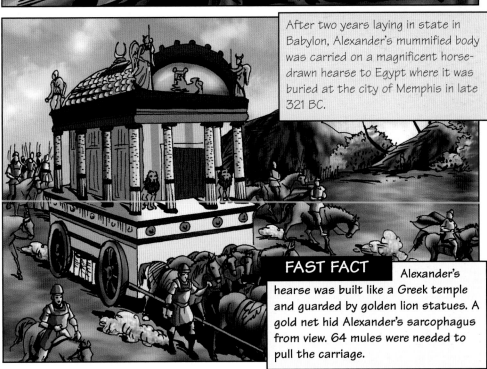

After two years laying in state in Babylon, Alexander's mummified body was carried on a magnificent horse-drawn hearse to Egypt where it was buried at the city of Memphis in late 321 BC.

FAST FACT
Alexander's hearse was built like a Greek temple and guarded by golden lion statues. A gold net hid Alexander's sarcophagus from view. 64 mules were needed to pull the carriage.

Alexander's short but spectacular life was full of adventure. He fought many battles over such a big area, and was involved in endless plots and murders. Inevitably it is impossible to include everything in one book. This timeline and fast fact section fills in some of the gaps in Alexander's extraordinary life.

July 20, 356 BC: *Birth of Alexander.*

343: *Alexander taught by Aristotle at Mieza.*

340/339: *Alexander regent at Pella in Philip's absence.*

336: *Philip assassinated at Aegae; Alexander becomes king as Alexander III.*

335: *Alexander fights the Triballi tribe in Thrace, and the Illyrians.*

334: *Alexander takes command of the invasion of Persia and crosses into Asia.*

May 334: *Battle of the River Granicus.*

September 334: *Alexander takes Halicarnassus.*

Spring 333: *Alexander campaigns in Phrygia, and cuts the Gordion Knot.*

November 333: *Alexander fights and defeats the Persians at the Battle of Issus.*

January-August 332: *Siege and eventual destruction of Tyre.*

November 332: *Alexander enters Egypt and is welcomed as Pharaoh.*

January-March 331: *Alexander visits Siwa Oasis and is welcomed as 'Son of Ammon'; Alexander founds Alexandria on Egypt's Mediterranean coast.*

1 October 331: *Alexander defeats the Persians at the Battle of Gaugamela.*

October-December 331: *Alexander marches south to Babylon, Susa, and Persepolis.*

May 330: *Alexander burns the great palace at Persepolis.*

Spring 329: *Alexander crosses the Hindu Kush to Bactra.*

Summer 329: *Capture and execution of the pretender Bessus.*

November 328: *Alexander murders Cleitus the Black at Maracanda (Samarkand).*

Spring 327: *Capture of the Sogdian Rock; Alexander marries Roxanne.*

Winter 327: *Alexander re-crosses the Hindu Kush and invades India.*

May 326: *Alexander defeats the Indian Rajah Porus at the Battle of the Hydaspes.*

June 326: *Macedonian army mutinies and Alexander decides to return to Babylon.*

Spring 325: *Alexander near fatally wounded while assaulting a town of the Malli tribe.*

September/October 325: *March through the Gedrosian desert.*

April 234: *Mass weddings of Macedonians and Persian women at Susa.*

June 324: *Macedonian army mutinies at Opis; Alexander reconciles them.*

October 324: *Alexander's close friend Hephaestion dies in Ecbatana.*

June 10, 323: *Alexander dies in Babylon aged 33.*

DID YOU KNOW?

 1 *The Kingdom of Macedonia in northern Greece was composed of thirteen regions. Macedonians spoke a rustic dialect of Greek, and were considered rough and unsophisticated by the Greeks of Athens and Thebes.*

2 *Alexander's father, King Philip II, made Macedonia into a powerful imperial state. He set the stage for Alexander by conquering the southern Greek city-states, and ruling them in his role as Hegemon (leader) of the League of Corinth.*

 3 *Determined to punish the Greek city-states for rebelling while he was fighting the northern tribes in 335, Alexander laid siege to Thebes. After his victory he destroyed the city completely as a warning to others.*

4 *Alexander's most dangerous enemy in the early years of the invasion of Asia was the mercenary Greek general Memnon who fought against the Macedonians until his death in 333.*

5 *In 334, after his successful siege of Halicarnassus, Alexander adopted the city's former Queen Ada as his honorary mother. He appointed her governor of the whole region of Caria, and left his general Ptolemy with her for a year.*

 6 *In November and December 331, Alexander stormed the mountainous lands of the Uxii, breaking through the so-called Persian Gates and then marched on Persepolis.*

7 *One of Alexander's most spectacular victories was his 326 capture of the almost inaccessible Rock of Aornus in what is today northern Pakistan.*

8 *In July, Alexander's former treasurer Harpalus arrived in Athens with a vast amount of gold and silver he had stolen while Alexander was in India.*

9 *Alexander had Hephaestion's body mummified at Ecbatana, but cremated his remains at a huge funeral in Babylon in the summer of 323, just weeks before he himself died.*

 10 *In the months before his own death, Alexander planned for the invasion of Arabia by building a huge fleet of ships and converting Babylon into a great river port.*

11 *Murder conspiracies circulated in the weeks and months after Alexander's death. Some believed that Alexander's own cup bearer Iolaus poisoned Alexander's wine, while others consider a conspiracy of the top generals a possibility.*

12 *After Alexander's death, his generals fought a bitter struggle for the succession. In a daring coup, Ptolemy hijacked Alexander's embalmed body at Damascus in 321 and buried it at Memphis in Egypt. It was later reburied in Alexandria.*

Aegae: *Original Macedonian capital before Pella was built. It became the sacred burial ground of the Macedonian kings. King Philip II, Alexander's father, was murdered in its theatre.*

Alexandria: *Officially Alexandria-by-Egypt, founded by Alexander in 331 BC at the western extreme of the Nile Delta. It became the largest and most successful of the many Alexandrias that Alexander created.*

Ammon: *Greek form of the Egyptian god Amun, sometimes joined with Zeus, king of the Olympian gods in Greece.*

Aristotle: *Famous Greek philosopher (384-322 BC) whose father had been the royal doctor to King Philip's father, Amyntas III. Alexander sent Aristotle specimens of plants and animals from his Asian wars.*

Babylon: *Great city built on the banks of the rivers Tigris and Euphrates in Mesopotamia (modern Iraq). Surrounded by double walls and featuring eight gates. Dedicated to the local god Marduk, Babylon was where Alexander died on 10 June 323 BC.*

Bessus: *Satrap of the Persian province of Bactria. He murdered his relative King Darius, was captured by Ptolemy and executed by Alexander in 329 BC.*

Chaeronea: *Famous battle in 338 BC between the Macedonians under Philip and Alexander, and an alliance of Greek cities led by Athens and Thebes. Notable for bringing to an end the independence of the Greek city-states.*

Chiliarchy: *A unit of 1,000 men in the Macedonian army.*

Cleitus the Black: *Macedonian nobleman who saved Alexander's life at the Battle of the Granicus. Alexander murdered him in a drunken brawl in 328 BC.*

Cyrus the Great: *Founder of the Persian empire (559-530 BC) who died still fighting to expand his realm near the Caspian Sea. He was buried at Pasargadae, near Persepolis.*

Darius III: *Persian king who confronted Alexander. He had assassinated his predecessor Artaxerxes IV, but is often regarded as incompetent in his dealings with Alexander.*

Dionysus: *Greek god of wine and excess as well as of disguise. Alexander and his mother Olympias were keen followers of Dionysus's religious cult. Dionysus's mythical adventures in India inspired Alexander to outdo him.*

Gordion Knot: *An intricate knot that was tied to the funeral hearse of the mythical King Gordius, at the Phrygian capital of Gordium. It was said that anyone who could untie it would rule Asia. Alexander slashed it with hi sword, and the prediction was fulfilled.*

Hephaestion: *Intimate friend of Alexander from childhood to death. The two men were likened to the two Homeric heroes Achilles and Patroclus.*

Hoplites: *Greek infantrymen who carried round shields and spears.*

GLOSSARY

Marduk: *Chief god of the Babylonians whose great stepped temple, dominated the city's skyline.*

Nearchus: *Born in Crete, Nearchus was a childhood friend of Alexander who later became Admiral of the Fleet in the voyage down the Indus.*

Olympias: *Alexander's mother and a princess of the neighbouring kingdom of Molossia. She was cruel and spiteful, and may have behind the assassination of Alexander's father, King Philip.*

Parmenion: *Senior general of the Macedonian army under King Philip, and then again under Alexander. He was murdered after Alexander had his eldest son Philotas killed for treason.*

Pella: *New Macedonian capital built in the 5th century BC. It became a sophisticated imperial capital under King Philip II.*

Persepolis: *Ceremonial capital of the Persian empire. It was built by King Darius I and his son Xerxes, and destroyed by fire at Alexander's command in 330 BC.*

Phalanx: *The line of infantry arranged for battle.*

Philip II: *Alexander's father who transformed Macedonia from a backward region into a premier league military state through army reforms and a string of military victories.*

Porus: *Tall and fearless Rajah of the Punjab region in India. He fought Alexander at the Hydaspes river and was retained after his defeat as an ally of the Macedonians.*

Ptolemy: *Macedonian noble and childhood friend of Alexander who accompanied him across Asia and was rewarded for his loyalty and fighting skill by being made a Marshal of the Empire. After Alexander's death, he became king of Egypt.*

Roxanne: *Bactrian princess who became Alexander's wife after his victory at the Sogdian Rock. She gave Alexander his only legitimate heir, Alexander IV.*

Sacred Band: *This was a group of 300 Theban warriors who formed into 150 pairs of male lovers and who vowed to fight to the death at the Battle of Chaeronea against the Macedonians. They are commemorated by a great marble lion statue that still stands.*

Sarissa: *Long infantry spear invented by King Philip and a deadly weapon in the hands of well-drilled army units. It was 5m long and held in both hands.*

Satrap: *Greek version of the Persian word which meant provincial governor.*

Siwa: *Large desert oasis in Egypt and home to the sacred oracle of the god Ammon. Already famous before Alexander's time, it was consulted by him in 332/1, and ever after he regarded himself as the divine son of Ammon.*

Susa: *The administrative capital of the Persian empire where records were kept in the cuneiform script incised onto sun-dried clay tablets. Alexander staged his mass wedding between Macedonians and Persian women here in 324 BC.*

INDEX